Money Around the World

Earning Money

Rebecca Rissman

www.heinemann.co.uk/library
Visit our website to find out more information about Heinemann Library books.

To order:

 Phone 44 (0) 1865 888066

 Send a fax to 44 (0) 1865 314091

 Visit the Heinemann Bookshop at www.heinemann.co.uk/library to browse our catalogue and order online.

First published in Great Britain by Heinemann Library, Halley Court, Jordan Hill, Oxford OX2 8EJ, part of Harcourt Education. Heinemann is a registered trademark of Harcourt Education Ltd.

Editorial: Diyan Leake
Design: Joanna Hinton-Malivoire and Steve Mead
Picture research: Tracy Cummins
Production: Duncan Gilbert

Origination: Chroma Graphics (Overseas) Pte Ltd
Printed and bound in China by South China Printing Company Ltd

ISBN 978 0 431 02524 7
12 11 10 09 08
10 9 8 7 6 5 4 3 2 1

British Library Cataloguing in Publication Data
Rissman, Rebecca
Earning money. - (Money around the world)
1. Wages - Juvenile literature 2. Labor - Juvenile literature
I. Title
331.2'1

Acknowledgments
The author and publisher are grateful to the following for permission to reproduce copyright material: © Alamy p. **19** (Peter Titmuss), © Corbis pp. **17** (Stock This Way/Hill Street Studios), **18** (Atlantide Phototravel); © drr.net p. **16** (Keith Dennemiller); © Getty Images pp. **4** (Bruce Forster), **6** (Andrew Hetherington), **7** (Zubin Shroff), **9** (Gavin Hellier), **10** (Michael Blann), **11** (Cancan Chu), **14** (Margo Silver), **15** (Jose Luis Pelaez Inc.), **23a** (Bruce Forster); © Masterfile p. **12** (Jerzyworks); © PeterArnold Inc. pp. **13** (Martin Harvey), **20** (Jorgen Schytte); © The World Bank pp. **5, 8, 21** (Curt Carnemark), **back cover** (Curt Carnemark), **23b** (Eric Miller).

Cover photograph reproduced with permission of © Alamy (Jon Arnold Images).

Every effort has been made to contact copyright holders of any material reproduced in this book. Any omissions will be rectified in subsequent printings if notice is given to the publisher.

Contents

Earning money

People work to earn money.

People do all kinds of work.

When people work, they are paid.

They are paid money.

Selling things

People sell things to earn money.

People sell things to eat.
People sell things to use.

Some people sell bread to
earn money.

Some people sell fruit to earn money.

Some people sell houses to earn money.

Some people sell pots to earn money.

Selling services

People sell services to earn money.

This means they do jobs for
other people.

Some people's job is to cook food for others.

Some people's job is to clean
for others.

Some people drive buses to
earn money.

Some people deliver mail to
earn money.

Money around the world

All around the world, people
earn money.

How would you like to earn money?

Ways to earn money

Things people can sell to earn money
- fruit
- clothing
- toys
- DVDs
- books

Things people can do to earn money
- care for people
- babysit
- serve food
- drive buses
- clean houses

Picture glossary

 **earn** get money for work you have done

 **work** what people do to earn money

Index

Notes for parents and teachers

Before reading

Ask the children what jobs people do. Explain that people are paid money for doing a job.

After reading

• Set up a role-play area as a work place such as a garage with mechanics, secretaries, and sales people. Encourage the children to play in role and to use money to pay for goods and services.

• Make a chart of jobs children might do around the house such as picking up toys, feeding the pet, and helping to wash the car. Invite the children to discuss how much each job is worth; for example, picking up a sock = 1p; feeding the pet = 20p. Talk about the way that the bigger the job is, the more money you earn.

• Tell the children to make up coins to the value of 10p in as many ways as they can.